THE ATTIC SAINT

To all mothers.

To my wife, the mother of our children, and co-author of our best "stories."

To my own mother, who first read books like this to me and gave me a love for language and stories.

And to Our Blessed Mother, for her role in the greatest story ever told.

—T.D.

Emmaus Road Publishing
1468 Parkview Circle
Steubenville, Ohio 43952

Library of Congress Control Number: 2019952382
ISBN: Hardcover, 978-1-645850-15-1; Paperback, 978-1-645850-16-8; eBook, 978-1-645850-17-5.

Design and Illustrations by: T. Schluenderfritz

THE ATTIC SAINT

By Tim Drake

Illustrated by T. Schluenderfritz

EMMAUS ROAD
PUBLISHING

Steubenville, Ohio
www.emmausroad.org

L EO AND HIS PARENTS had just moved to a
        new house in a new city.
        To be more accurate, it was an *old* house in
an *old* city, but it was new to Leo just the same.

In the beginning, Leo didn't much like his new home. It was very large—larger than the two-bedroom apartment he was used to—and it was unlike any house he had ever seen.

His mother said the house had "character" and "charm" and that he would grow to love it.

Leo wasn't so sure.

It seemed to Leo that the house was full of squeaks and creaks. The oak staircase complained every time he went upstairs or down, and the old doors reminded him of screaming mice whenever they opened.

The basement was the worst.

Once, his father asked him to go into the basement to fetch a tool.

Leo felt a chill as he walked down the steep steps and brushed against the cold gray stone wall. The air was damp, and the smell reminded him of dirt.

To Leo, it seemed as if the house was far too dark. Especially the living room. It seemed to get very little sunlight.

A large painting decorated the living room wall. On second thought, it didn't decorate the wall; it merely hung upon it. The painting reminded Leo of being sick.

"Mom, what is that painting supposed to be?" Leo often asked his mother.

"I've told you before, honey, it's an abstract," his mother said. "It can be whatever you want it to be."

But no matter how many times Leo looked at it, he didn't think it looked like anything at all.

Leo's father said that the house had once been a convent—a place where nuns lived, worked, and prayed.

On sunny days, Leo would sit on the front step and imagine what life was like when the house was full.

He pictured neighborhood children playing on the sidewalk and imagined nuns in their flowing habits of black.

Swish . . . they floated by like passing ships.

In time, the house started to grow on Leo. There were things that he began to like. He liked the silly squares that sat above the doorframes. The circles inside the squares reminded him of wagon wheels.

He liked the warmth of the radiators. He could set his socks on them to warm his feet.

But most of all, he liked the upstairs library. It had something that no other room had: stained glass windows!

In the silence of the afternoon, while his mother napped, Leo would lay on the rug and read. As the sun began its descent, the windows would cast moving images across the library floor.

One day after lunch, while Leo was reading, the dove in the stained glass window appeared to fly across the library floor toward the stairway that led to the attic.

Leo decided to follow it.

The attic was dusty and warm and fragrant with the smell of very old wood. From the ceiling, bare light bulbs hung on twisted cords. To Leo, it looked like the inside of an old Viking ship.

From the attic's large window, Leo could see his entire town and even the mountains beyond.

Except for a few boxes, the attic was empty. So, with little to explore, Leo left the attic, slamming the door behind him.

Bang!

A loud noise came from inside the attic as he started down the stairs.

"What was that?!" Leo wondered.

Frightened, he decided not to go back inside . . . at least not right away.

But later, Leo gathered his courage and revisited the attic. As he opened the door, a sliver of sunlight reflected off of a bit of gold. It caught Leo's eye. To his surprise, he found something that had not been there the day before.

Just inside the door sat a rectangular piece of wood with some writing on it. Leo walked over to take a look.

As he did, Leo realized that it was no ordinary piece of wood. Leo stared at the kind face and large eyes of the stranger on the board. He seemed to smile. There was something different about this image because it felt to Leo as if the man was gazing at him.

"Where did this come from?" Leo asked himself. "Why didn't I see this yesterday?"

Looking up at the attic's wooden rafters, Leo wondered if someone had tucked the board away up there. When he had slammed the door the day before, the image must have fallen.

As Leo studied the face, he exclaimed, "I've never seen a picture like this. I wonder what it is?"

To Leo, it almost seemed as if the figure spoke to him.

"It's a holy form of prayer—an icon. Some call them windows to heaven."

The voice frightened Leo, so he left the attic and returned to the library.

But he kept thinking about the image and that *voice*.
He could not seem to get it out of his head.

Two days later, Leo returned to the attic.

"Don't be afraid," the deep and friendly voice seemed
to say. It reminded him of his grandfather.

"Who are you?" wondered Leo.

Taking the image in his hands, he noticed the
handwritten letters. It read

SAINT AMBROSE

Saint Ambrose? "What's a saint?" asked Leo.

"A saint is someone who loves Jesus very much and who now lives in Heaven."

"Well, it's good to meet you," responded Leo.

Just then, Leo became alarmed.

"Oh! a bee," he exclaimed.

For a bee had gotten into the attic and was sitting on the icon, buzzing.

"Bees have always liked me. When I was a baby, honey bees landed on my face and left some honey on my lips, but I was not harmed. This foretold that one day my words would be sweet, like the bees' honey."

The more Leo looked at the image, the more questions he had. While there wasn't a lot of light in the attic, it seemed to Leo as if light radiated from the gold and the colors in the icon.

"How am I able to hear your voice? It's like you're alive."

"In a sense, I am," responded Ambrose. *"Icons are made of living things: wood of a tree, egg yolk, vinegar, water, and color pigments from plants and minerals. An icon brings all of creation together."*

"Why are there crosses around your neck?" Leo asked.
"*I have crosses around my neck to show that I am a Christian, a follower of Jesus Christ, the Son of God.*"

As Leo continued to study the icon, he noticed other things in the painting.
"Why are you wearing such strange clothing?"
"*I am a bishop of the Church. My clothes are called vestments. They are the clothing of a bishop.*"
"What's a bishop?"

"A bishop is someone who has been selected to be a shepherd, guiding God's flock to Jesus."

"And what is that book that you are holding?"

"It is the Bible—the very Word of God. We come to know Jesus by reading about him in this book."

For the next few days, Leo continued his afternoon visits to the attic to spend time with the icon. During their visits, Leo learned much more about Ambrose.

"*I never wanted to be a bishop,*" Saint Ambrose told Leo.

"In fact, I was a lawyer and judge in Italy—the country that is shaped like a boot. But one day the former bishop of my city, Milan, died, and a fight broke out over who would replace him. I went to the election and tried to calm down the shouting crowd.

The assembly became very quiet, and then the voice of a child rang out: 'Ambrose for Bishop!'"

"The crowd yelled out in agreement.

I ran and hid myself at the palace. After all, I was not a priest and hadn't even been baptized. I tried to get help from Probus, the Head Governor of Rome, but he said I would make a perfect bishop.

Eventually, I realized that this must be God's will, His holy purpose, for my life. Within seven days I was baptized, ordained a priest, and made Bishop of Milan. I gave away my land to the Church, sold my possessions, and gave the money to the poor."

Leo's questions continued.
"Why are you in the attic?" he asked.
"I used to hang on the wall in the living room."
"Well, what happened?" asked Leo.
"A previous family felt I had outlived my usefulness.
They could not relate to a man from so long ago."

Leo wasn't exactly sure what Saint Ambrose meant, but he couldn't leave the icon alone anymore. He picked up St. Ambrose, tucked him under his arm, and swiftly carried him downstairs to his bedroom.

At dinner that evening, Leo shared the painting with his mother and father.

"That's quite a treasure you've found," said his father.

"Can we hang it up, Dad?" Leo asked.

"Well, I don't know. … I'm not sure we have a place for a saint," his father murmured.

"Oh, please Dad, please? I know just the spot for him."

After giving it some thought, his father replied, "Well, if it was painted in the house and left in the house, I guess it deserves to stay in the house."

After dinner, Leo led his father to the living room. He stopped at the empty space on the wall near the coat closet.

"Right there!" pointed Leo.

"Perfect," his father said. "It looks like that spot was made for the picture. Let's hang it up right away."

To their surprise, a very small nail head already marked the spot where the icon came to rest.

From that time on, Leo's visits to Ambrose continued.

Once, his mother thought she heard him speaking to the icon.

Soon, the whole family came to prefer Ambrose to the abstract.

Leo wasn't sure why, but he felt that the icon somehow changed the room—and the entire house. To Leo, the house seemed brighter than ever.

"Let your door stand open to receive Him,
unlock your soul to Him,
offer Him a welcome in your mind,
and then you will see the riches of simplicity,
the treasures of peace,
the joy of grace.
Throw wide the gate of your heart,
stand before the sun of the everlasting light."

—ST. AMBROSE—

Tɪᴍ Dʀᴀᴋᴇ once found a religious painting in an attic. He serves as executive director of Pacem in Terris Hermitage Retreat Center. An award-winning author and former journalist, his books include *Behind Bella* and the children's coloring books *Viva Cristo Rey!* and *From an Angel in a Dream.* He resides in St. Joseph, Minnesota with his wife and children.

Tʜᴇᴏᴅᴏʀᴇ Sᴄʜʟᴜᴇɴᴅᴇʀғʀɪᴛᴢ once lived in a former convent. He is the illustrator of several books including the Old and New Series by Maura Roan McKeegan, *A Life of Our Lord for Children*, and the *The Book of Angels.* He is a freelance graphic designer and the art director for *Catholic Digest* and *Gilbert Magazine*. He lives in Littleton, Colorado with his wife Rachel and children.